Free Range

POEMS

Teresa Nan Travis

BOOKSIDE Press

ISBN: 978-1-77883-133-1 (Paperback)

        978-1-77883-135-5 (Hardback)

        978-1-77883-134-8 (E-book)

BOOKSIDE Press

BookSide Press
877-741-8091
www.booksidepress.com
orders@booksidepress.com

Contents

Ignis Fata - Faerie Fyre

Our days pass too swiftly for our keeping
Dreams are the shadows of their flight
We review them in our sleeping
Fabricated from the colors of our sight…

Sometimes stars speak in strange voices
As they spin upon the wheel of night
I paint the dreams I never dream
My pen gathers them to write
So here are a few—I made for you!
As gifts for your delight.

A Note Found Under The Carpet

(Found by Menelaus, King of Sparta – three days later)

To Helen,
A ship awaits with diamonds on its oars
And a crimson sail
To take us from this dark shore
We ride the emerald waves
Upon a dolphin's tail.

Throw back thy head in laughter
Fling back thy golden hair
Our ship is calling
Come with us if you dare!
Come away from drudgery and duty
To travel by the stars
To live in freedom and with beauty
Far from the thrones of Minotaurs.

Fabled cities now await us
We, together, side by side
I will be thy lover
Thou, my fair young bride!
With a wind to fill our sails
The wind we call the Tramontine
On the dappled waters of the Adriatic Sea…

Beloved Helen,
Do not worry
Troy is invincible

With seven fortress walls
Revels and dancing,
Joyful music in her halls
Attar of jasmine and wild roses
Will perfume thy golden hair
Clothes soft as moon beams
Thou shall always wear.
As we lie on scented pillows
As they feast us everywhere.

No garlic breathing old Greek husband
Who treats thee as a servant
Will annoy thee anymore.
Forever, the Greeks must quarrel
Forever, they must destroy!

Lovely Helen –
Wrapped in woman's duties
Obedient and coy
Bare thy breasts of beauty
And come with me to Troy!

Come to our ship tonight
Bring thy women and thy dowry
The Greeks will never catch us
In our sudden flight.
Fear not for thy safety
Our ship is fast and tight.

Helen – my golden treasure
Be my queen in Troy
Thou costly gem of pleasure
Be a queen in Troy!

Our ship is leaving on the next tide
If thou choose to come with me
Make haste now to decide.

Signed,
Paris, Prince of Troy

A Socialist Society - Socialists

Ants live in cities. They have streets and boulevards.
They have a good economy because they work so very hard.
Ant engineering build tunnels, ant farmers milk aphid cows.
Ants have state nurseries for the ant children
No ant is unemployed.

Monarchists

Bees are royalists by custom and regime.
Every bee is a prince—child of a Queen.
Bees dance among the flowers to tell where they have been.
They dance to tell the other bees about the blossoms they have seen.
Bees have banks with hexagonal vaults
Where they story their golden honey
(which is an edible sweet form of money.)
Every bee is industrious and free
Their work is to supply food for winter
They collect pollen—not for themselves alone, but for the hive.
They work for their survival to keep their community alive.
Sometimes bees swarm, but in winter
They cluster together to stay warm.
The Queen has many suitors—suitors are called drones.
The Queen never flies alone.
All the bees follow her
Wherever she makes her new hive and home.

Men live in cities which is a people zoo.
They work nine to five and jobs are all they do.
People would be happier—humans could be free.
If they acted like the busy ant or the dancing bee.

A Wizard, Raven, And A Tree

In the world's misty morn
When the world was being formed
Even before the human race was born…
There came a ragged wanderer—most forlorn
He—a Wizard came to northern shores unknown
Where he etched his runes on crags of stone
Tooled by antler, writ with bone
As he roamed wide and far alone
With no cave or den to call his own.

Upon a rugged mountainside
Where trolls and sea-dragons still abide
The fjords rise steep on narrow cliffs
With secret sigils, signs and glyphs
His work was making magic spells
Secrets of lost treasures tell
Long ago and forgotten
As lost as the ocean's heave and swell.

The Wizard spoke and divided time
Into infinite circles that around us bind
Solstices and Rituals of the Equinox
Following ancient ways of Eagle, Wolf, Bear, and Fox.
The Wizard spoke a living word within his veins
As gnarled fingers twined with twisted limbs,
His worn-tattered clothing of rough skins
His face hidden by tree-bark masks
Or masks of woven leaves…

He could see all—but none see him
As he climbed primeval trees to sleep unharmed
Gigantic trees cradled him in their shaggy arms.
Hidden by the vines that dangled down like fetish charms
Among the dunes and bogs and tarns...

Where lived the trolls, giants, and the Norns
He dwelt with all of them among...
But the Tree named Yggdrasil was his favorite one
In the shaded forests—on the living breathing Earth
Trees are the Planet's lungs.

Yggdrasil Tree was by the Wizard
His dear and most befriended
This was his tree that the Wizard often tended
Yggdrasil—the mighty tree
King of the Forest, so vast was he,
Of profound wisdom from his antiquity.
So slowly had this tree grown
That a thousand years passed as one day to him
Yggdrasil's top reached up to Heaven's dome
Upheld regions of Gods and heroes—all well known
But below—down deep below
Among Yggdrasil's roots were the caverns of Death's Goddess Hell
Within the Court of the Demon Dead was Herself enthroned...

The Wizard reached out to climb to a higher vault
—his hand broke a thin branch which flung him like a catapult
Plunging and spiraling as he fell
(Like those whom by ambition stray from Nature are compelled)

Still hundreds of feet above the ground
But midway down
In the Midgard world of humankind
He remains until Ragnarok or The End of Time.

The Wizard had carved Yggdrasil with many runes
There in the branches of Yggdrasil he swooned…
The sun left the sky, no bird rejoiced
No star cold flames lit the sky with orphaned moons.
In fevered dreams his mind was consumed
By lost memories and dismal thoughts of doom.
The Wizard hung for many stark raving nights
Extinguishing the summer's exquisite light
Ravaged by storms,

Chilled by the winds
Their freezing bite
Savaged and torn by winter's spite.

To high branches the Wizard clung
Bound by Yggdrasil twisted within vines
As if vine were ropes and cobwebs twine.
His head down towards the Earth hung
Back and forth he swung.
By the winds just like a pendulum.
By the arrows and spears of rain—he was stung…
Nine dark – nine starless nights
Savage clouds at him were flung
As if by the anger of the Norns
Who extinguished all of his hopes and his delight
His beard and brow were stiff frozen white
His mummy wrapped body shrouded and quiet.

Bitter winds blew on the winter ice.
There he made blood sacrifice
Because—every wisdom hath its price.

On Yggdrasil his blood flowed—his soul descended
His Spirit to the Cold Court of Hell
There he surrendered to her spell
The tree was his witness and defense
To the Great Goddess Hell
The Queen willed the Wizard with her to dwell
But his Soul was lifted up thru the great hearted tree—
His Soul within the tree rose up within
the tree his self was blended—
With Yggdrasil—by the Tree of Life—Spirit ascended
By sap of Yggdrasil—the Wizard's Body mended.

Ravens perched on his shoulder and in his beard
To peck out his eyes which were rolled back and weird...
But his sudden revival the ravens feared
When the corpse jerked upwards suddenly
The craven birds quickly withdrew
In feathered flurry
Hopping away in a measured hurry.
Stealing body parts from Wizards—well might they worry!
One bold ravenous Raven had already eaten one eye
One Half of the Wizard's own light.
Brazen bird had stolen half of the Wizard's sight.

Ravens—who once sung songs so sweet
Now in raucous voices—his hoarse call meet
From that day—a croak is all the Ravens' cry

(Now you know the reason why…)
Crass are Ravens and their brothers, the Crows
(As everyone already knows)
Crow and Raven are brothers—both are clever thieves
(For this is written on the most common leaves.)
Raven alone is obliged to be the Wizard's own spy.
Cursed is Raven who stole a Wizard's eye
Now half of the year in the Northland is in darkness
The cold of Hel reminds all of the Wizard's keen distress.
So… When the world is dark and the Raven you hear,
Be grateful and do not fear.
A ragged old wanderer—a one-eyed stranger, perhaps is near
Wearing a slouched hat, with a tangled gray beard…
Once called Odin, All Father, Master of Runes
As ancient as Earth, the Sky, the Sun or the Moon.

He has one cyclopean eye that have circles within circles of Infinity.
Just like the circles on the stump or on the trunk of a tree.

15

(About Wolves)
(Taking the protected status of "endangered" away from wolves.)

The shadows below, under a full moon in white.
The haunted woods are pitch where the wolves howl on a
narrow ledge. They howl beyond this world to the windy
valleys below. It's a sound like all the grief that has ever been
felt by any soul who has suffered—a cry for the hunted
and murdered. Beloved mates and brothers each precious
friend remembered and now no more. No more.

A cliff looms high, hill-born and tempest wise… Like a castle
without gate, windows, or a door, that nature carved and built of
orphan stone. Pillars rise with great mossy arches etched in arcane
alphabets—the rocks like ancient runes. Here—we drink the
champagne of solitude, reflect upon fierce streaks of meteors, the
swirl of silent planets in a sky's star-lit flames, temples to forgotten
gods where prayers are leaves in flight. Hours die on the tears
of the morning—the invisible as Immortal Being unknown.

Winds echo the cry of wolves—unheard by man in his glory. Men in
high offices with tall black glass windows, shining brilliant electric
lights, revolving doors. Human ears stopped by self-righteous
indifference. Humans don't hear the weeping of wolves in the night.

Wolves cannot know why they are hunted and killed by men with rifles, poisoned, or trapped. They wail to a world beyond time and beyond this world. A song echoes far away from the night. Crying to a world beyond this world—where the Invisible listens... and feels the pain in their hearts. The Invisible feels all things done and undone. Hears the prayers like leaves in flight where hours die on tears of the morning.

Absolutely Scientific!

Using logical deduction
Obtuse terminology
Long equations
A mile of statistics
Strict experiments and tests
We have conclusive evidence
That it's just a wild guess!

American Doors

Super-security
Paranoid doors
Electronic spy doors
Secret code doors
"STAY OUT" THEY SHOUT
"WE ARE IMPORTANT DOORS!"
With surveillance cameras
Boxes with tinny recorded voices
No way! Go away!
Keep out!
Trespassers Will Be Eaten!
No Soliciting, No Skateboarding, No littering,
No Smoking, No Diving, No. No. No.
WHERE are the signs that say:
"REQUIRED LOITERING"
"PARK YOUR ASS ON THE GRASS"
"FREE BEER"

What's behind door #2?
Zilch
What's behind the plastic curtains?
More plastic curtains?

Has the U.S. become a bank vault?
Lock out the strangers,
Block out all the dangers.

NEW AMERICAN SIGN READS:
Cowardly Rich People Live Here
Check in with the Armed Guards
For permission to visit the self-made prisoners.

Afraid of giving.
Afraid of sharing.
Afraid of living.
Afraid of dying.

Anal Retentive Doors
Everything shoveled in
Making sure nothing trickles out.

These Doors.
They are not doors but walls.

Battle Of The Red and Black

Red-tailed Hawk and Raven Black
In Spring compete for the best nesting place
Among the ancient skulls of rock
High nests safe among the craggy cliffs,
Upon the angled mountain face.

Red and Black
Red and Black
See the Dance, the Battle.
Beat the Shaman drum
Shake the gourd and rattle

Red-tailed Hawk screams on high
Soaring wings sweep a wild sky
To challenge the Blue Black Raven
With a fierce and fearless cry.

Then comes the raucous Raven
Arrives the Raven nigh
Answers with a hoarse and homely caw
To stake his claim to a high domain
To rule by his own law.

For the mountain tops, they battle all the day
In flight their skill and artistry display
Red and Black, Red and Black
See the Dance, the Battle.

Beat the Shaman Drum
Shake the gourd and rattle.

A steel beak and talon claw
Red-tailed Hawk
Rides the swift coursers of the wind
With outstretched wings to block
Raven, thief of eggs, that bold outlaw
The thief of nesting straw.

Silent Stranger of the Night
The Great Horned Owl,
Has come to watch
The Hawk and Raven fight
He sits upon the pole to observe
Maneuvers of their flight
Like a judge aloof, aloft
His head first swivels to the left
Then it swivels to the right
One eye blinked off to ponder
His other eye is wide and round with wonder.

Comes the rabble – Jays to scold and scoff
Call all the bets each side
Disdainful of the matter.

Red and Black, Red and Black
See the Dance, the Battle
Beat the Shaman drum,
Shake the gourd, the rattle.

Each Spring – the Red and Black
Dive and dip in flight
To defend or to attack
They often scream and cry
They do not kill each other
Nor do they even try.
They fight for a nesting place
And the dominion of the sky.

Blues For Pinnochio

When you were new
The world was your stage
And everyone loved you
Such a special puppet
Such a cute wooden toy.

You still blame Gepetto
But he is just an old man
Without a magic wand
Gepetto carved a wooden puppet
But love made him a father
But love could not create a son.

All day you hang there limp
Dangling all your strings
Although you admire the blue fairy
(You say she has pretty wings)
You never listen to what she says
Or listen to the lyrics
When the blue fairy sings.

Any cricket could tell you
Who you really are.
You do not know you are Pinnochio
You think you are the star.
But your circus has no acrobats
Just one pathetic clown
Wearing a painted smile

Or a perpetual frown
Depending on if you are right side up
Or if you are upside down.

Are your feet so broken
You can never take a stand?
Can you ever help another?
When you never lend a hand?
Will you mouth your same lines forever?
Your words already spoken
Words you do not understand
Like a record broken…
Honesty takes a real boy.
Forgiveness makes a real man.

Bodhisattavas Drifting Leaves
(Tibet Invaded By China)

Bodhisattvas drifting leaves
Stolen from the Bodhi Tree
Painted clouds in saffron silk
A tan dakini in bikini
Dipped in Pearl, draped in milk
Gleaming like a precious metal
Pouring tea from a copper kettle.

Dakini with a gentle sigh
"Who will catch those leaves for me?
And put the Bodhisattvas back on the tree?
A dragon's eye now burns my skin
While the winds are pale and thin
The night is cold and my heart is dry
Treasured gold turns to tin.
When there is no enlightenment to win."

A Poison Arrow Emerald Frog
Squats upon a lotus log
Staring at plump peyote dog
This barking boy, and laughing God.

Vermilion Sun, a Dragon's Eye
Saffron moon trapped like an amber fly
Days like sailing ships go by
Wind walkers spinning high

Froggie hears the Dakini's cry
Intoxicated by celestial sound
Emerald Frog bounced round and round
Staring upwards from the ground
He vows – He'll bring the Bodhisattvas down.

So up and up he climbs
To a tossed and tousled limb
He smiles with a Cheshire's grin.
His eyes are fat, his cheeks are thin
He is the Jester, King of Thieves
To capture all the falling leaves
And glue them back upon the tree.
Bodhisattvas on a Boddhi Tree.
Meditation –their Monastery
Wings of chants – so light and free
Butterflies on the Dharma Sea.

Butt Cleavage: Sex Symbol of the Post-Industrial Age

Your bedroom is a ghetto.
Your brain has been surgically removed
To make room for the implanted cell phone.
More metal studs and your tattoos.
Your mouth is a sewer
Your biggest emotion is outrage
Your high school prepares you for prison
Your home is a temporary cage.

(Chorus)
Butt cleavage, butt cleavage
Let that flabby ass hang out
Butt cleavage, butt cleavage
You know what it's all about.

Your girl's cosmetics are applied by Earl Schibes
Her two-tone lipstick crackles when she smiles…
When she struts down the street
She sets off car alarms for miles.

(Chorus)
Butt cleavage, butt cleavage
Let that flabby ass hang out
Butt cleavage, butt cleavage
You know what it's all about.

Your boom box is registered on a seismograph
A demolition derby—or a piled up car crash
You stand on your hood to play your air guitar
Only problem is—you ain't going very far
Because your girlfriend slashed your tires
After you set her green hair on fire

(Chorus)
But cleavage, butt cleavage
Let that flabby ass hang out
Butt cleavage, butt cleavage
You know what it's all about.

Celtic Morning - No Caffeine

When the Romans left—the British Celts were devastated.
They were observed wandering around Stonehenge
In a lost and forlorn way.
Who could they revolt against?
No one to trick or petition. It was depressing.
Would they have to go back to being barbarians again?
The good thing was all the best spas were now vacant.
The druids who weren't murdered by the Romans were back.
But someone was keeping secrets
Probably that pesky little Wizard—Merlin.
Merlin wasn't even a Celt, he was a Pict.
Celts liked venison, but there wasn't a deer anywhere to be found.
The forest was razed around Stonehenge.
There weren't even enough sticks to make a campfire.
All the trees had been used up.
But rocks were plentiful.
Deer don't eat rocks.
Fortunately, the Celts still had all their natural teeth.
Because sugar hadn't been invented.
Wild tattooed Picts remained in their caves up North.
Whenever people chased them
Suspicious rabbits ducked into their tunnels.
Boring, moralistic priests
Tried to make them feel bad.
Their wives and women joined up with the sissy Christians
And people gossiped about a sword stuck in a rock.
To have a contest to see who could pull it out?
The lucky winner would become King.

(Celts hated Kings. Kings collect TAXES.)
Dutifully, they all pulled on the sword—
Grunting, sweating, and cussing.
It certainly seemed stuck!
Then one day, a freckled, buck-toothed, rascally kid
Stole the sword from the rock.

They all rolled their eyes and said "Now what?"
NO RAIDS, NO NIGHTCLUBS, NO CAFFEINE, NO SUGAR.
And the Christians were going to ruin everything!
Good thing—they still had the Saxons and Viking hordes to fight.

Dancing On Broken Mirrors

We dance a dance on broken mirrors
With bleeding feet and timid mind
Dance a dance of puppets
On mirrors of the blind
Images so bright and sharp
But image all we find

We dance a dance of broken mirrors
With lagging feet and common crimes
We close our eyes
Inside us is another mirror
Where we find
We are prisoners of our prejudice
The investment of our lies
By the opinions that we ourselves opined
All we see is ourselves
But we are not the self we see.

Reflections are reversed
The way mirrors are designed
Left is right
And right is left
Before is just behind.
In shattered mirrors
We multiply the images
And brightly magnify the shine.

Intoxication and confusion
Which face is the face of Self Divine?
Fascination with illusion
Is this yours or mine?
Blinded by reflections
The clamor of the bright
Devotion or desperation
We are all hypnotized by sight.

Sweep away—this broken mirror
Repeated imitations
Without jagged edges
And the fractured line
No limitations
Nothing to confine.
No Gods, no roles to play
One Alone
Invisible, Immeasurable
The soul unknown
within us all
The heart—our only home.

Farewell

Daughter—gather up the blankets and the food that still remains
Put it in the satchels—Take the spotted
horse—He is the one most tamed.
Before you is a long journey—many dangers—
Until you reach the warriors of our tribe.
The dogs of war are coming—the soldiers will soon arrive.
You must cross the canyons—far to the other
side—look for secret signs …
Swift clouds chase the thunder—
I hear the drumming hooves of the ghost buffalo
Sky Brother sends us a signal—it is time to go.
Do you remember the caves and caverns—
Where our people lived long ago?
Paintings and carvings in the high cliffs above
For the Echoes—Spirit Voices—to speak to the tribe below.

Now the sky is shadowed—the light grows dim
The new moon is—a knife blade—sharp and thin.
Ride, daughter, ride! To your freedom
That you may live in our sacred ways.

"Oh, Mother…won't you please come with me?
I will put the blankets on the spotted pony…
We will walk beside him when he is tired.
In the light of day—we will hide.
I will hunt rabbits and bring them to our fire.
Please come—Mother
Or…let me stay here with you.

I will fight the dog soldiers until they kill us.
I will fight with my knife and spear.
Mother, I will stay beside you.
See—I have no fear.

No, Child, I must stay.
Go swiftly and go safely now
I pray.
Your dreams and visions
Guide you on your way.
Keep thy Spirit strong
Because to the future
Does thy youth belong.

The Farewell

Farewell today—soon forgotten
There are many greetings
Along your way.

Oh, Mother
I feel as if I shall weep forever,
Like the winter sky.
Will I ever sleep in your arms
Or listen to your stories
Hide behind your skirts again?
Knowing that your life you give
To defend my life,
You die—that I may live…

My daughter
As the sun rises in the morning
To darkness—it must descend.
All that begins—someday must also end.

Your pony will lead you to the water,
Trust him and follow.
… Wisdom be your Scout,
May Spirit lead you .

We are one
Within each other…
Within each other

Earth Mother—Bless your daughter,
Be her most loving friend!

We are smoke that mingles
In our soul's sweet blend.
Spirit never dies
Love can never end.

Flame of Love

Let the flame of love
Burn the fire of violence
Let fire be healed by flame.
Let cool waters of compassion
Heal the flood of tears…
Lest we scorch in hell
And drown ourselves with sorrow
For those we did not love
For those we did not help.
And pray, children, pray
For all that we cannot love
For those we cannot reach.

Glastonbury

Once I was a traveler
I wandered the roads along
I was a student minstrel then
A-gathering my song.
The strangest sight
Was midsummer's night
In a place called Glastonbury
Where (I swear it's true)
I saw at closest view
The trooping of the Fairy.

Dancing in the long twilight
Was a horned man dressed in furs and skins
His naked arms and legs were painted all in blue.
He danced for twenty hours
From dawn to dusk to dawn.
He danced a hunter's dance
The whole midsummer through.
As he danced
All the people danced
And I danced too!
The very same dance as he!

Above us lost in clouds
Was an ancient broken tor
Legend says—it is the place where
Queen Guinevere is buried.

Above the tower, ravens circled round
By the high drafting winds
All these great wings were ferried.
Suddenly—the mountains glowed

All eyes wide and dazzled
So struck by astonishment
Our song ceased and music slowed
And Eldritch folk marched in a line before us
T'was the trooping of the Fairy Host
They looked real and not like ghosts
But from whence they came
To where they disappeared
We shall never know.

Tall princely men in hunting cloaks of brown
Slender ladies in long silver gowns
Auburn tresses hanging down
Leaving no footprints on the ground.
So sweet and solemn faced
No human knows such noble grace
Much taller than this modern race
Much to my amaze
Yet how we too could be.
As in this holy place
Where storm and rainbow have given birth

They appeared and disappeared into the hollow
Where no mortal feet can follow
It has been decades since I was there
And for years I was afraid to share
As I began to compare…

Modern men live for comfort and convenience
We live the safe lives of sheep and cattle
What truth can we ever know
When we wear the bit and bridle?
We think ourselves alive
While we walk the pale shadow.
Let the wildness be reborn within us
To dance the Blue Man's dance
For equinox and solstice.

Modern man has lost his faith
Modern men have sold their souls
Turned belief into a cynic's scorn.

On high the same stars shine
The stars shine so clear and cold
Summer lightning flashes
Distant thunder rolls
There is joy and wonder
Which comes from days of old.

Wear your eyes like silver
Wear your smile like gold.
See the same stars dancing
As in the days of old.

By the flickering firelight.
A spiral is dancing into flight.
Silver swans are winging
Over violet pools of sky.

Green winds are singing
Waters broken by reflections
Of a million laughing eyes
They are all around us—watching
You may have seen them in their disguise

What is a future made for us by robots and machine?
If you know not who you are or where you've been?
Reality has roots like a tree
The honored ancestry of hoof and horn,
The tree contains the sap of all that's holy—all that is born.

Gospel Country Rap Song

I'm a cosmic surfer
On the cosmic sea
I wiped out
Sharks surrounded me
Jesus is the lifeguard
Won't you rescue me?
We'll hang ten
To the beach of eternity.

I'm a cowboy
On the lone prairie
And I'm lost in hostile Injun territory
There's an Injun behind every tree
With automatic arrows
Pointed at me.
Jesus is the cavalry
Lord let me ride with thee
Back to the fort of eternity.

I'm in jail for a felony
But I swear Lord, that it wasn't me.
The Devil D.A. says he's got me on the nail
But I know Jesus already raised my bail.
Judge, oh, Judge not me!
Jesus is my lawyer
He'll set me free
To go home to my family.

Meanwhile…
I'm calling collect to eternity.

I'm a dancer on the street.
I'm smiling at everyone I meet.
Sister, you can have my seat.
Cause I got the rhythm and I got the beat.

I'm dancing up to the thirteenth floor
I'm knockin' on Heaven's door.

St. Pete – look at my shoes – how they are wore.
And my feet are mighty sore
Jesus is my cobbler.
He repairs the soul I tore.
I'll dance for Jesus forever more.

Guess Who Came To Tea?

I sat in the parlor A white napkin on knee
Buttering the toast
Sipping my tea
In calculated disregard of his animosity.

I called him "Ernestine."
(Just to be mean)
"What's my name? What's my name?"
Spitting in my face as he screamed…

Now—I pride myself on being a good hostess
(A ridiculous thing, I confess…)
So without raising an eyebrow, I asked
"Tea"
"Would you prefer lemon? Or cream?"

"Alright, back to the business at hand…
Is it Owen? Could it be Sam?
Gustavo, Odin, or Shelley
Sure, NOT…Josephine?"
I smiled sweetly at him
(Nasty little Goblin…)
We were never properly introduced.

You see… I was in a bit of a pickle once.
It was a business deal…(well, I had no choice.)
And he was here to collect…
Unless I could figure out his name…
(And what would HE do with a baby anyway?)

Unfortunately, for the poor ugly creature,
He drinks hard liquor
And dances around his barbeque in the woods
Snorting and braying…like a jackass!
Fortunately,
I enjoy exploring those very same woods
And I heard his name plainly
But I kept it to myself—for the moment.

"RUMPLESTILTSKIN!" I said
(Trying not to snicker, but smugly triumphant)
He looked so confused
(I almost felt sorry for him)
I explained…"I THINK I WIN!"

Now I sit in the parlor
White napkin on knee
Watching the children
Sipping my tea…

There is a broken statue of a goblin
Squatting at the edge of the garden
(An amazing resemblance to him)
The little Princes often play with it
Until suppertime, when I call them in.

Jacumba Spa

Curved thin scalpel of moon
Sliced the evening sky in perfect quarters
(sectioned like an orange)

Landscape of night spread out before us
Framed by peripheral shadows of trees
The luminous green velvet water
Stars magnifications above
Sparkling micro-fields within...
Dancing a billion molecular dances...
Interwoven with tails of comets
Skidding around corners of the universe.

Summer streams of consciousness
Conversations
Shots of smooth golden tequila.
Moon hooked like a scalpel
Dissecting landscapes of night.

Life On Planet Dirt

I dust and clean almost every day
But the dust never goes away...
The broom makes the dust to fly
Up my nose—into my eye
And turns into mud—if I should cry.

My vacuum cleaner blows
It will not suck
In reverse I fear t'is stuck.

Someday when I die
The dust will cover my bones
Wherever I lie
But I'll be in a celestial hotel
On the Milky Way
With room service every day
Leaving dust on earth to stay.
STAY DIRT STAY
Brown and grey
On clean laundered clouds
I'll sail away.

Love And Desire

Love and desire are dreadful masters.
To little love is shown
And much too much is said.
They are houses built of playing cards
Which stand and fall alone.

Of love I will seldom speak
My opinion what does it matter?
If that is what you seek
Then be careful
Of who will kiss you on the cheek.

There are many loves
Of youth and lustful fire
As earthly seasons go round and round
Snow quenches Spring's desire
Restless winds have blown away
The harvests that were sown.
We might go to buy the fruit
That in hothouses are too quickly grown.
Hearts are stolen
The heart that we have never known.
Life lives on in flesh and blood
With rotten pits and maggots in the stone.
Forgotten is the place we never see
Where the heart is free.

All the things and people
We can never own.
Every house whether large or small
Is never our true home.

Love and fear have many names.
Motives have many masks and faces.
People play so many games
Custom has so many places.

Love will beckon the rootless, reckless heart
It tangles feet that go astray
Idle pleasures and pretense
In shallow waters play

A goal (even a worthy one)
Will lead you by the nose.
Where your success or failure
Are deep waters that will flow
If you cannot swim, you'll drown
No matter where it goes…

But all in all
We forget the place
The place we never see
Where the heart is free.
All the things and people
We can never own
Every house whether large or small
Is never our true home.

Love of A Winter Knight

In the long darkness of the Northlands
Lady Borealis garbed in colors
Flaming hair of layered light
Blue, green and golden bands
Among the fairy courtiers
She is the airy sprite.

Shimmering in satin gowns
Among freezing pavilions
Dancing rondelets and rounds
The Blizzard Queens in jeweled tiaras
Boreal Kings in diamond crowns.

High Court of Stars and Moon
Scintillating splendors, breathtaking tapestries of frost
In a glacier palace with bright crystal rooms…
There the Lady Aurora Borealis is greeted by the Winter Knight.

"I have watched thee, Lady, dancing in the air
I thrill to see thy leisured step
Gliding unconcerned
Ascending and descending bright celestial stair…
Give me leave to speak—one moment please, I pray
Blissful Borealis—for one moment stay."

Startled shy, Lady Borealis drew her skirts away
Made as if to go, then capricious fey
She turned again to say:
"Speak freely—Sir Knight,I listen."
(Their eyes meeting friend to friend)

Icicle wands sparkle, glisten
In the ice caves below.
Glassy rooms of Glacier Castles
Spired in the snow.

The Winter Knight he said:
"I am an old harsh Warrior
Without thy artful vision, I am blinded by my darkness
You are so light; you give my eyes—their sight.
I would thy champion be—if thou consent to spend one night.
To spend this one night with me."
The Knight implored His-One adored:
"Lady Aurora Borealis, light me with thy fire.
Save me from the deep so cold
Thou art my heart's delight
Darling of my soul."

Replied the Lady Borealis
"Dark Knight, Sir Thunder-Drummer
Warrior—harsh and cold.
Thou hast won my favor, with thy words so bold.
I glimmer bright—this Arctic night
For thee I dance the long twilight.
Thou—my scarf of many colors wear
I'll wrap thee in my waving hair…

Come into my chambers, Lord,
Take off thy silver armor.
Unbuckle steel sword
Be this night with thy amor,
We are of one accord."

"Make haste,
We must not waste
Our few precious hours.
The pleasure of thy company,
No greater troth than ours."

There upon a cloud-curtained bed
Linens of the finest weave draped with moonlit snow
She pulled him down with her bright sleeve
She wound her necklace around his great head
With a many colored glow.

Sequined stars on piled velvet sunk into the azure deep…
Within a lighted circle
Aurora curls round in the Knight's arms asleep.
Metal fists knock upon the shutters
Skeletal fingers tap upon the glass
Unholy bitter winds, chords about the Castle Keep.

Within the vaulted glacial chamber—a Lady's arms are summer
Flowers of her streaming hair
A Knight watches over his Lady's slumber
Envisions Springtime in the air.
Aurora Borealis (within her dreams)—she smiles.

Quiet embers of the winter fire
Soft glowing with late raptures of desire
Then Lo…
The flashing sword of solar ray
Parts the horizon's curtain of swollen clouds
With unwelcomed dawn.
Then tiptoed in the mundane day
Flashing its white-toothed grin
The dark must fade—as day begins
As Winter yields to Spring.

Knight gently wakes his love to say:
"Oh, Lady of the Courtly Dances
Indulge thy Knight once more.
With a final kiss—one more sweet kiss
Our bliss is swiftly gone…
Farewell, My Lady Borealis."
The Knight departs…
His sword to buckle on.

Metamorph

Who journeys miles of smiles
Across the freedom of the sky?
A lowly worm, the caterpillar
Emerging from its silken shroud
Cocooned therein to lie
Until the Resurrection day.
It emerges with patterned wing
Shaking them to dry
An insect angel
The fair and fragile butterfly.

From caterpillar, spinner of cocoon
To someday be
Dressed like a flower
Yet more free.
It floats and flutters by
Through clouds and over trees
Swept by the wind
And each passing breeze
Dancing, glancing,
With graceful, joyful ease
It may fly to far distant lands
Without a map, leader, nor any plan.

Guided by faith called "instinct"
A scientific word
Used by man for what he does not understand.

At the end of the long journey
To the place where they must die.
They put their two front legs together
Tiny hands together raised as in prayer...
They lift their bodies up
Arched into the air.

The butterfly does not decompose
It simply dries.
Then as glittering fairy dust,
Blows into the skies.
Caterpillar to cocoon to butterfly.
A message of metamorphosis
That death we may transcend
When we raise ourselves in prayer
In order to ascend.

By faith alone to be guided
Never knowing how or why
With beauty and with joy
Upon these wings to fly.

Mistaken Identity

Sometimes I see myself
As someone I once knew
A mistaken identity
Of the first degree.

Nose to nose with mirror
Whom do I see?
The face—it seems familiar,
So I check my own I.D.

I know who you think I am,
And what you think I thought.
You told everyone—you knew me well.
But stop. I'm not.

I am not a bit like you.
However, you may be
Someone a bit like me!

Moonless Night Sky

Tonight
The moon has drowned
In a river of jewels.

Stars are swimming laps
Across
Infinite silence.

My Neighbor Is A Camel

(About Refugees In America)

My neighbor is a camel
He's not a cigarette
He is the first camel that I've never met.
My neighbor, the camel, lives next door.
I never had a neighbor who was a camel before.
My neighbor is the only camel on my block
He's a foreign camel so he doesn't like to talk.
My neighbor is a camel
You'd never guess he is a rising star
He plays the bass on an electric guitar.
He sings homesick songs about the desert sand.
On Facebook, I found out he is the leader
Of a Dromedary Band.
(They say he has a lot of fans…)
He's not a wealthy camel who lives like a Sheik
He drives an old jalopy, and calls himself Mike!

My neighbor is a camel
He's not a cigarette.
They say camels spit
But he never spits on me.
I'm not prejudiced against camels
I'm prejudiced against smelly cigarettes.

Ode to Toad

Evening yawned—pale as pretty cakes
Creeping across the armored plates
Fat and sleepless naps
Wide-rounded Toad

A picnic cloth is his abode.
"Wherefore ploppest thou, Oh Mighty Toad
Upon thy warty road
With dishy spoon and bristled fork?"

Grinning Toad Declares:
"The time has come for pantry work
Now is not a moment's shirk.
Gather for the feastly food
Or business find me—in a beastly mood!"

Hosting Toad
Traffics the swarming insect throng
As they vagrantly picnic among
He herds and hurries them along.
For those who hurry—will not wait
For the ones who vacillate.

Most Genial Toad
Welcomes even those arriving late
He clears a place for them upon his plate
Brushing off the crumbs to seat their dates.

How Toad Attends the Ants:
Oh, hear them clamor!—How they cheer!
Some crazy ants swim in left-over beer.
Soon to be drowned, alas, we fear!

Toad Conducts Chorale
Musical Mosquitos,
Shrill high soprano song
Toad directs them with baton
Declaring that their key is wrong.
But Toad's instruction—heed they none.
Until he taps them gently with his tongue.
One singer into the silence gone
The next Diva-mosquito comes along.

Toad's Work
Festivities are over but never done…
Until
The belch of beaming sun…
And tired Toad plops into bed.
When the Zombie Ants rise from the dead.

Off-Roading From The Straight And Narrow

Polka-dot pants and a pink umbrella
Lots of rouge and lots of mascara
Don't care is a dame is a fella.
Cause we're off-roading the straight and narrow
Gonna have fun tonight.

You feel fine and I feel bettah!
When you wear that tight sweatah!
We're off-roading the straight and narrow
Gonna have fun tonight.

No need to fuss or fight
No need to be uptight.
Cause we're gonna dance all night
We're off-roading the straight and narrow.
Gonna have fun tonight!

Shimmy, shimmy like my sister Jimmy
Shake and bake like my cousin Jake.
We don't care if your boobs are fake!
We'll dance all night, What a sight!

Polka dots and a pink umbrella.
Off-roading the straight and narrow.

Overheard: Erudite Discussion In The Trees

Three sophisticated monkeys were talking under the jungle canopy… They were brunching on bananas in their favorite tree.

First monkey asked: "Is it true that humans
are related to us, to you and me?"
The second monkey said: "Humans are a barbaric
species—more destructive than a chimpanzee."
The third monkey picked and ate a flea…
"Man is a parvenu—They smell peculiar, the
appearance is frightful, and so bad tempered too."
Third monkey agreed: "Yes, men are savage,
violent, they often disagree…"

First monkey said: "Men are afraid of insects—
terrified of a harmless bee."
The second monkey: "Humans are inhibited by gravity… Man is a
pedestrian species that walks down on the ground because they don't
have tails—they cannot swing from the branches of a tree…" The
three monkeys considered this with pity as they shook their heads…

The first monkey added: "Although there may be a few
characteristics we share since all of us are mammals in no
way do humans compare to a monkey's superiority."
The second monkey said: "I infer that man is no
distant relative. We have nothing in common,
therefore they cannot be related to such as we."

The monkeys concluded: "Humans trespass upon our forest—where they steal our babies, they put us in cages or eat us... They are cannibals—primitive creatures— they lack our good manners and our morality."

Purpose

If you have a passion for excellence
No other competitor is as tough
When the impossible is your greatest challenge
Your best is never enough...
With purpose—you must have a plan
Without action—it's only wishful thinking
Your heart is where you take your stand.

Work hard on each detail
Until skill is at your command
If at first you fail—don't worry
Try again and again—if you can.
Know your worth—don't be inflated
Expecting high rewards you have not earned.
Pride will soon be dissipated
By all the things, yet unlearned.

Put past mistakes behind you
From previous folly comes mirth.
Follow good advice and don't argue
Some'll always reject you
But at the end—you'll be happy
To see your work is well done.

Quero

I dreamt of a grave
It kept filling with water
That year the sickness took my brother,
My baby, and my daughter.
The grave was filled with my sorrow.

My daughter saw my brother
Her uncle who had died three months before
"Oh Uncle—do not leave me here alone."
She closed her eyes—she went away from our home.

We wrapped her in her bridal dress
In her arms we placed the toy she had loved the best
Her smooth raven hair covered her breast.
We covered her face
In her wedding lace.

Then the baby became ill,
We were working in the potato field
My wife took care
But there was no help anywhere.
So the baby died.
My wife wrapped the baby in her own woven shroud
She dug a grave with her hands
Weeping aloud.

My brother lived high in the mountains
He knew the Akis and Apus

In those Spirits—he believes,
There he prepared a sacrifice
He burned the holy coca leaves.

The alpaca and llamas
March around him
With tinkling silver bells
My brother drinks chi-cha
And shares it with the llamas
They were drunk as well

When my brother died
He was playing his flute to the wind.
He said to me,
"I live in the Andes, high above the jungle flowers,
These stones are my fortress and towers,
I play the flute to pass my long lonely hours.
I play for my herd, I play for the Akis and Apus,
I play for our fathers—that the wind will hear.

When I die—let the condor pick the flesh from my bones
Let my bones bleach white in the sun
Until they are cold as the moon.
Make a flute from the bone of my thigh.
Grind my fingers to dust and place the dust in my skull,
Drink the chi-cha from my skull.

Play a song for me that the winds may hear.
For I journey to the land of our fathers
To play them my song.
The winds will remember."

Requiem for Children of the Wind

The stallion to his harem calls
The herd panics in confusion
He rears as his closest companion falls
A high powered rifle shot
The smoking gun
The Stallions ears lie flat to fight
The herd screams in fear
Ready to stampede and run
But imprisoned by the blinding light.
The horses are shot down
They fall screaming to the ground.
The Men beat and bludgeon the wounded ones
With iron clubs and guns
Men spray fire extinguishers in the horses' eyes
Horses are driven to their knees
In bloody anguish some for hours lie
White eyes blindly staring at the sun.
Over the bloody massacre
Only the vultures fly.

What victory is won by violence?
What death worthy of the price?
In the dust – a symbol is dying
Who gains by this bloody sacrifice?

Roads of Life

Sands in hourglass
Are leaking thru
The days pass—as they must do.

The world changes lanes
It goes too fast and I am too slow.
I stop to let the traffic thru.

We come, we go.
Nothing lasts except the flow.
The more the changes,
The less we know.

The more roads they build,
The less the view.
How strange to see myself
Just passing thru!

Solitude

I set forth upon my journey
My destination I knew not
For knowledge I studied
By experience I was taught.

I had many dreams
Disappointment was my lot
Every love was a sacrifice
What was it that I sought?

Was my life a futile investment
In a future cemetery plot?
Whom had I ignored?
Who was the one whom I knew not?

Who is the teacher of my soul?
What is the inspiration of my thought?
My longing in the beginning
My solitude at the end.

I realize that within my loneliness
Is the home of all, I, now befriend
Solitude is a quiet Angel
It is the pilgrim's flame.
It is the inner temple of my heart
It is a path without a name.

Song Of The Crystal Angel

One small Angel dwelt with Almighty God in Heaven
Lived in eternal bliss
Then the Angel went one day to visit Planet Earth
So was charmed at first.
As the Angel watched
The world went from good to worse
The little Angel witnessed pain and sorrow
In which the world was immersed.
So the Angel returned to God...
And this is the Angel's story:

"When I saw the Earth suffering,
My lips would not ope to sing
And so I prostrated myself
Before my Lord and King.
My silence seemed an accusation
To the Creator of Everything.
But when I saw the Earth's suffering
My songs I could not sing...
And so my Lord was angry
He pulled off my soft feathered wings
He took from me my eyes
And my lips that would not sing
Banished then from Heaven
Down to the Earth to dwell
Silent and blind
Into the Earth I fell.
Deep into the darkness

As I plunged and turned
Meanwhile back in Heaven
Back inside the Prism
The White Light coldly burned.

I lived a million lifetimes
Among fissures in the mines.
I was stressed and pressed by gravity
To many gemstones I gave birth
Crystals are a fallen Angel's teardrops
As I wept beneath the Earth.

One day I was found by a man
He chiseled me from stone
As he hit and pounded me
I began to sigh and moan.
One of my eyes – it opened wide
I saw I was a crystal
Translucent, hard, and clear.
When I looked at the man
He ran from me in fear.

I was on a city street
Where people waved fronds of palm
The crowds waved sheaves of wheat
For a man riding a white donkey
His face was sad and sweet.
When he passed close to me
He smiled at me
Suddenly I was filled with light.
It was my Lord and King

His face was human
His eyes were shining bright
And I saw his terrible suffering
So I began to sing
I sung a song more beautiful
Then any song I ever sang before.

And as I sang…
My wings grew back upon my shoulders
Above the world I began to soar.
I sang a song of Love
To the Holy One that I adore.

Surfer Jesus

Jesus walks on water
He doesn't need a board
He looks like Captain Nemo
But folks just call him Lord.

He usually wears sandals
And he has a beard.
Preachers say he is not a hippie
Although he is rather weird.

Jesus's pals are Buddha, Krishna
Pals from long ago
Because all the Saints are surfers
One with the Cosmic Flow.

The ocean swell is splendid
Waves are glorified
But when you surf with Jesus
Your soul is sanctified.

The Impatient Patient

Doctor Scorpio told a terrible tale
A story of a patient who received a bill in the mail.
A silly mistake—the receptionist made
When she sent him a hefty bill unpaid.
She sent him a possible prognosis for a rare tropical disease
(his name circled in red) Cure unknown, he thought it said.
Drop a check in the return envelope—if your please.
Well, he was staggered. His sanity fled.
He sat for hours, his hands on his head.
Considering that he was soon to be dead.
He was sure a quick death
Was preferable than lengthy suffering and to die slow…
An option—seemed to him a better way to go.
He searched for his pistol through his underwear
A pistol—he had never had the opportunity to use before.
He locked all the doors and began to prepare.
First he cleaned the pistol, loaded the chambers.
Put the gun to his temple,
Pulled back the hammer.
Then he pulled the trigger.
CLICK
It's a jammer. Go figger!
In frustration he tossed his pistol behind the incinerator
Twirling in air, the pistol blew, as if in compensation for the jamming
Bullets ricocheted everywhere.
Wounding a refrigerator, nicking the blender
Fatally punctured a toaster,
There was a shocked silence for a minute or two.

Then with severe annoyance, they hissed as distressed appliances do
In electronic defiance.

Well, the man was so upset that he had missed
He thought he might slice his wrists.
But it so happened—he was fresh out of razors that day.
Knives in the sink were too dirty
He might get an infection that way.
His electric razor had safety features
It wasn't sharp enough anyway.
So he decided to jump out the window.
He relocked the doors, closed his eyes, and leaped
Unfortunately he lived on the ground floor.
Landed in the flower bed, many petunias were crushed.
A fat nosy neighbor was watching.
She asked him, "Why don't you use the door?"
She snickered: "After all, that's what they're for!"
She scolded him with matronly disapproval
"Just look what you've done to the petunias!
"Don't ever do that again! Understand?"
He hung his head and nodded
Backing out of the flower bed—he plodded
Dusting off the dirt clods from his rear-end.
Stammering excuses—all phony and lame.
Like a sinner caught sinning, his face flushed with shame.
He promised not to crush the petunias again. (a futile promise)
In his endeavors to end his own life,
The poor man rushed to the train station,
To wait for the train,
But the train never came.
He waited in vain.

While lying down on the track
After a few hours—it began to hurt his back.
He arose from the tracks and began to complain.
A bystander—a cheerful woman was glad to explain.
"Those tracks haven't been used for years, my dear.
Not since Lord knows when… Try those other tracks over there.
Anyhow, you missed the last train. It left at half past ten.
Come back tomorrow if you like and try it again."
She bid him good evening… He didn't smile back

He was upset after his long hard day on the tracks.
The poor man was a wreck.
His glasses hung from one side of his nose to his neck.
His bow tie was looped over his ear.
His hair stood on end.
He looked mighty queer.
His arms swung around his bony knees.
Shoulders slumped in defeat.
It was strange because he had always looked so dapper and neat.
When he turned to go home
He realized he had locked himself out.
He looked for the fat neighbor, he hid in the
bushes, until she wasn't about…
Watching and waiting until he felt sure she was gone…
So he could climb back through the window,
The same way he got out…
He slunk past the manicured lawn and
back over the petunias again…

Remember?—I told you his promise was in vain.
As he swung a leg over the window sill, he heard her shout!
He tripped and fell on his elbow—screamed in pain.

He cursed and whimpered—tried not to cry.
He didn't want HER to notice tears in his eyes.
He limped to the sofa and sank down with a sigh.
Plugged in the T.V.
POW! Fizzle! Sizzle and **POP!**
Some kind of short.
(A warning to NEVER EVER aggravate your appliances—
If you value your life!
People! Be kind to your appliances is our sage advice.
Don't abuse a toaster, don't cuss, or threaten a microwave
With a gun or a knife.)

THE IMPATIENT PATIENT (or the revenge of the appliances)

Of course the man wasn't dead,
He was sent to emergency room instead.
When he woke up—he had no eyebrows
He was bandaged from his feet to his head.
He was strapped into a hospital bed.
The nurses wouldn't bring him a bedpan or turn on a fan.
By his bandages he was disguised—was he Zombie or man?
Doctor Scorpio went to visit his patient
His medical condition to inspect.
The doctor took all his vitals—his blood pressure he checked…
Then the patient grabbed the doctor's arm.
"Doc, I'm so glad you came!"
Doctor Scorpio looked at him with alarm.
"Doc, can you tell me if the rare tropical disease causes much pain?"
Doctor said: "What rare tropical disease?"
The patient gave him the hard-to-pronounce long Latin name.
The doctor listened and after a chuckle he explained…
"That's a Latin quotation for a delinquent debt overdue.

Might hurt your wallet, but that's nothing new.
If you don't pay—we could always use spare parts from you.
We'll stick you back together with crazy glue.
Your brain—you wouldn't miss it and I promise NO PAIN!"
Then Doc smiled" "Don't worry. It's a free
operation—if you are broke.
(This is Doctor Scorpio's typical medical joke.)

Finally discharged—the patient went home.
Trembling—to face his appliances alone.
Afraid to turn on the light,
He stumbled around with a candle—all night.
He moved out the next day.
The fat nosy neighbor reported that she saw him in a taxi
As it sped away.
She said he didn't say goodbye or even wave.
He is grateful for his life and not yet fit for his grave!
But he paid his bill—the receptionist said.
Oh,… HE paid his doctor's bill – oh yes.
But he left no forwarding address.
No one has seen him in a while, I guess.
We wish him good luck, good health, and all the best…
We hope he feels much better and has gotten over his distress.

The Magistrate's Daughter

Adrian was a bold gypsy
He was daring and free
Adrian was the best horsemen
In all the border country.
No man could catch him
To hang him from the gallows tree.

The Magistrate said the Gypsy stole horses
But the truth was—he only stole me.
I was the Magistrate's only daughter
Spoiled, reckless, and free.

Adrian was called "King of the Gypsies"
With his winnings of races
He fed all the children of the Romany
Hated and feared by the town folk
Despised by my own family.

Adrian came to town riding a black stallion
I rode my father's finest white mare
Although my father refused to allow it
Together we rode in rebellion
To win a prize at the fair.
My father's white horse sure of winning
Until the Gypsy arrived
A fine golden ring was prize to the winner
With wagers of gold on each side.

The gypsy rider was dark and handsome
His horse was fleet as the wind
He swept up all of the wagers
Every prize and wager to win.
The gold ring he gave to the magistrate's daughter
With a sly wink and a grin
Then he stood in his stirrups and leaned over
And stole a long sweet kiss from me just for fun.
Had he known
I was the magistrate's golden-haired daughter
Perhaps he might not have done.

A passionate kiss took two hearts by surprise
The gypsy rider had taken more than the prize
For I was captured by his dark gypsy eyes
First love has seldom ever been wise.

I'd trade all the fine horses
I would give back the fine golden ring
For my life it means nothing
If I cannot have him.

The gypsies camped in a green glade
They lived in the deep forest shade
Where they hid their good horses
From envious eyes of the town folk.
Good horses which they race or will trade.
Horses for which a gypsy is paid.

I saw the old wooden wagons
Painted in gaudy colors
I saw the toothless old hags
I saw the poor gypsy children
Dressed in tatters and rags.
To them I was a stranger
They threw rocks to chase me away.

Unaware was I of the danger
I was always pampered and petted
And willful to get my own way.
I was the Magistrate's only daughter
Spoiled, reckless, and gay.
The gypsy children threw rocks
To chase me away.

A rock struck my horse and it shied
Then another stone hit my head
Down from the saddle I dived
My horse in panic it fled.
I fainted
When I awoke I saw soldiers.

My Gypsy Lover was dead.
The soldiers shot him
When he ran forwards to save me.
He held me in his arms as he died.
That is what the gypsies told me
That is what the soldiers all said.
The soldiers were paid by my father
Following the careless path I had laid.

I'd trade all the fine horses
Give back the fine golden ring
My life it means nothing
If I cannot have him.

I ran away from my father
It was no easy thing
To sleep in the forest
To weep over the grave of my lover,
My lover, the brave Gypsy King.

Crazy with grief, I was starving
I had gone out of my head.
The kind gypsies took pity
They healed my body and spirit
They brought me back from the dead.
I would not leave the forest
To go back to my father
No matter what anyone said.

I live with the Gypsies
Over my heart I wear a fine golden ring.
I race a black stallion
As sleek as a hawk's wing.
But I can never bring back the life of my darling
I cannot give back the life of their Gypsy King.

I race for the Gypsies
I care nothing for safety
I care only for speed
With all the wagers I win
The gypsy children I feed.

Someday he will come back to find me
Upon a midnight black steed.
I will follow my darling
Wherever my love will lead.

I would trade all the fine horses
I would give back the fine golden ring
I have nothing but sorrow
Because I do not have him.

The Midnight Ride of Alphonse, The Queer

Gather around folks about to hear
The midnight ride of Alphonse, The Queer.
When Alphonse's mother was pregnant she weighed 300 pounds
She thought she had gas for maybe the flu…
When she sneezed that day—out flew Alphonse too.
Alphonse was wearing pink diapers that day…
So everyone knew that baby was gay…

Alphonse grew up and bought a car called a "Yugo"
People said "You go ALPHONSE in your little "Yugo"
One midnight Alphonse was on the freeway
The Yugo had four cylinders, but Alphonse only used two.
He got caught in the fast lane
Going too slow
So he got rear-ended
All the way to IDAHO.

Ho Ho Ho! Did he return from where he had been?
Oh, NO NO NO.
What did he do when he got to Idaho?
He wore pajamas that were pink and red…
He took up Yoga
He stood on his head.
Until one day a moose hunter filled his fat ass with lead…
Now Alphonse spends his life in bed…
Making that moose hunter wish he'd killed him instead.

The Polyester Suit

A Polyester Suit came to Campo
Yes, it happened once long ago.
The word from Tecate to Pine Valley quickly spread
The locals shuddered with horror and dread…
A polyester suit in Campo?
How did it happen?" People said

The suit wasn't wild paisley
The polyester suit—at least it wasn't plaid…
But it was a Disney plastic color—definitely bad…
Poor Man!—the ladies twittered—perhaps it's some kind of fad.

Those who tell the story say the suit was luminescent green
It was only April—a long time before Halloween…
The boys at the bar elbowed and ogled…
Kids would stop and stare.
The POLYESTER SUIT INVASION
People were scared.

The boys at the bar snickered
You knew they were working out a plan…
Schemes were tossed across the table
Knowing looks from man to man…

The boys were up to no good.
The women could plainly see
At home there were words
Dogs would yelp and flee

Ears were fiercely tugged.
Children laughed in glee

Ducking from the pots and pans
That sailed across dusty yards into some spindly tree...
THE POLYESTER SUIT IN CAMPO
Was the subject on which families disagreed.

The ladies thought it was a sign of culture
Finally Campo had arrived
The guys were mightily offended
Real men wear t-shirts, blue jeans
Masculinity passionately defended!
LIFESTYLE or... DEATH—it seems...
Across Campo to Lake Morena Village,
Jacumba, Boulevard, Guatay, Dogpatch, Potrero, and Tecate.
Debate was hotly waged!

In the bar the boys drank beer—they were quietly enraged.
The Shitty Slicker in his suit walked into the bar
Oblivious to the impression that he made.
Big Leroy smiled his best shark smile—
Politely—offered the Shitty Slicker a stool
Shots of Wild Turkey passed around
Offers the Suit to shoot a game of pool.
People snickered to see
Which fool would play ol' Leroy
And the Suit was the victim they chose.

The Suit broke balls from scratch
The Suit let the balls fly
Nobody else got to the green felt table

As the Suit sent the eight ball down.
Amazed—the guys gathered around.
What do ya know…?
The Suit was a PRO…
But still his taste in clothes most hideous.

They toasted Polyester Suit
They drank to his health
They drank to his wealth
To his professional, but ill-gotten loot.
Spontaneous—the Annual Wild Turkey Shoot
They decided to make it deciduous…
So the guys took the Suit to the men's restroom
They stripped him down to his knickers.

NOW THIS WAS THE SHOCKER!
The Shitty Slicker had KNOCKERS!
It was an IT… not a guy.
A transvestite transsexual from Yonkers!
The cowboys slunk away…
To this very day… the guys won't say…
Whatever they saw… was against "natural law"
And their wives don't mention the "Suit" anymore.

But the "Suit" moved to Jacumba
Wears short shorts, tank top, nothing more.
Has lovely long wavy blonde hair…
If you ever go to Jacumba, you might see her there…
And The Polyester Suit still hangs in the thrift store.

The Proud Candle
A Fable

A candle claimed the fire.
It marveled at its own lovely glow.
The candle said, "This flame is mine," as
it basked in its own tiny halo.
The dark receded, as the light proceeded, to illuminate the room.
Everyone could see the candle, but the candle could not see itself.
The shadows grew restless in the deepest corners.
They drew together and grumbled.
A tiny breeze was wafting by…
It listened and heard the shadow's complaints.
Breeze sympathized with the shadows,
Because it too, being a breeze, was invisible.
Breeze knew what it was to be ignored, thus
becoming a mischievous draft.
Finding the crack in the window sill,
Breeze instantly blew the candle out.
The shadows danced with glee and mocked the waxen
Tears of the proud candle…
"See you are nothing but wax and wick…
You are not fire. You do not own the flame…"
The breeze winked at the candle and fled.
The candle bowed its head and was humbled in spirit…
Thus, the candle became more wise.

The Raven
(The Thunderbird)

The Raven is flying, He is flying high
He shatters the blue mirror
That blinded every eye –
Dark clouds are on his wings
As they come rolling by.

The Raven is flying. He is flying high.
The winds are the beating of his wings.
His shadow fills the sky
Far away the thunder drum
Echoes the Raven's cry.

The Raven is flying. He is flying high.
Dark clouds are his torn feathers
As he circles the wheel bye and bye.
But somewhere in the middle
The Raven's path will lie.

The Raven is flying. He is flying high.
He shatters the blue mirror
That blinded every eye!
See the lightning flashing
From His fierce and fearless eye.
Far away the thunder drum
Echoes the Raven's cry.

The Sun-King And The Priest

When the Spanish Priest held up his wooden cross
To the lips of the dying Sun-King he said:
"Renounce the worship of your heathen gods
And believe this black book."
He held it up for all the Inca People
To bow down and worship.
It tells the history of one tribe
And about one man who was killed
For being too wise.

Give up the worship of your Sun Star Lord
Who travels each day across the sky
Giving warmth, light, and life to everything
Freely shining on large and small alike
Faithful to the morning.
The Sun King of the Inca raised up his young dark face
He looked at the hawk-nosed Spaniard and the black book
With a sigh he looked once more into the skies
That he had studied so often.
He dropped his head. The Priest smiled bitterly
As the soldiers garroted The Royal Inca
As another heretic of the Holy Inquisition.

Lord knows his duty was done.

The Visionary Bear

Azure butterflies in spiral dance
Like wondrous flames of blue
With fragile wings, they dart and glance
Inviting old Shaggy Man of the Woods
To dance within their circle too.

Framing him
Like eyelashes of a lover's eyes
They flirt with easy grace
Old Shaggy Man enraptured
Nine-feet tall rising up he stood
With upward tilted face.
He raised each padded furry foot
And danced the best he could.

By Thy Love Be Sought

(For Big Steve Paden—my most perfect loving friend—a Saint)

Never forgotten is the true friend… Big Steve Paden
So many times I think of thee, best of all men I ever met.
Smiles and your sweet helpfulness
Thy gratitude, devotion, and humbleness…
In days of my own distress
Your comfort and shoulder—my pillar for duress…
Deeds, alone, all worth decides
No one here is deified
None suffered more than thee
No greater sacrifice than yours for me…
Loss of you was still a greater price…
When you died in pain, I was not there for thee…
Not at your side…as I should have been…
My dear, had I known your pain!
I would have laid down beside thee—and die for loyalty.
Were there more men in this world like thee,
A better world would surely be!
My friend forever you will always be.
You who thought yourself a monster!
In mind and soul, in truth I see the rarest gem, now lost to me.

Time Saving Technology

Without forethought
Off guard am caught
Whatever I am unprepared to do
I must do…
Of course can not.

Next
I return prepared
Armed with arsenal of tools
Instruction Manual
Diagrams and book of rules
Down upon my bended knees
See fine print in Japanese
Sweating – cussing – mostly praying
Trying to figure out what the book is saying.

Thing is not jammed
But tightly locked
And I forgot…
Where did I put the silly key…?

I think that I shall never see
Time that is saved for me
By Time Saving Technology.

To Sleeping Beauty
From the Prince

My Dear Beauty
I have finally found you
With a drop of blood upon your finger
And a smile upon your sweet lips
For a hundred years you lingered
In enchanted sleep
While all the tears that others weep
Are dry upon your cheek.
Did you not think to carry a thimble?
Perhaps you thought it was a joke
Evil fairy's reputed curse – ha ha!
Just some kind of hoax?

Of all the things
That a charming Prince might say
(My speeches well rehearsed)
"I'm sorry about your coma, dear,
And about that evil fairy's curse.
But you could be dead or paralyzed
It could be so much worse.
Did you ever dream of me?
Did I appear as a hero in thy dreams?
Did you realize, dear Lady
Your coiffure is out of style,
Your dress once elegant and fine
Is all faded now – antiquated in design?

Your blessings came too easily
Comfort came too cheap
You are a victim of denial
Your whole world is asleep.
You have a youth that never ripens
Mirrors reflect your fading grace
Idle years are passing
Thorns grow all around your place.

A hundred years have passed you by
On the spindle wheel of time
Since you were stabbed by a poison needle
Into the narrow circuits of your mind.
Now, of course strictly forbidden and illegal
Counted as a crime.

Oblivion like cold dark stones
Overcame my rivals – weak and unaware
Disappointed in their exalted expectations
Fearful of adventure, of dangers
They would never dare;
Judging others by their own limitations
By excuses that they fake…
All of them have fallen
Into that endless water
Into a shoreless lake
To rock in crystal waters
Never to awake.

I hacked my way through jungles
I whacked my way through dreadfully sharp thorns
Faint from hunger
My body bruised and torn.
As you lay comfortably sleeping
As a Princess born…

While I persevered through many tribulations
Through gale and through storm
I resisted the sexy sirens of temptations
Their kisses sweet – I scorned
The water was all poisoned
I almost perished there from thirst.
Then I heard you gently snoring
So I came to liberate you first.
To find out that you prefer your coma
Because you fear reality is worse…

All day you sit and watch TV.
You would rather watch commercials
Than to dance with me.
I am sorry, darling
You are a lovely corpse.
Pretty cadavers are everywhere, I find
I cannot kiss you, darling
I'm just not that kind.

Towers Of Babble

Towers of Babble in rubble they lie
While shadows of Shadrach threaten the sky
Old Testament cries "an eye for an eye"
So more innocent people can suffer and die…
Weapons are rattled with righteous outrage
Spotlights blind those on the stage
Until they run back to hide in their cage
History is repeated on the next page.

Metal monsters attack – blind on the run
Dust blurs the hot desert sun
The viewpoint is narrow from the scope of a gun.
Deaths are certain, statistics are none…
Media minions declare we have won…
Only traitors speak of damages done.

Patriotism is proudly displayed
Bless the bombs
For which YOU, taxpayers have paid…
Bless the easy profit from plunder they made.

Oh blessed are the lazy, the crazy, the salesman, the whore
Bless the rich who toil no more
Bless all you Patriots safe on the shore
While you send children of others
Out to die in your war.

War

Women weep tears of pity
Tears in torrents are shed
Men wage a war for their leader's ambitions
While women mourn for the dead.

The Grim Reaper again comes to harvest
To husk the flesh from the soul
Men believe they act for the best
But death is the price of man's toll.

Leaders receive all the glory
While soldiers into graves disappear
Unknown to the pages of history
While women weep every tear.

The leader to his people will call
Patriotic sounds a command
But the Chief is not there when you fall
To the Chief – you are a tool – not a man.

Leaders claim for themselves the grand victory
While soldiers in the fields disappear
A Leader claims the prize of the battle
Never the soldier's wounds or his fear.

Women weep tears of pity
Tears in torrents are shed
Men wage a war for their leader's ambitions
While women mourn for the dead.

Who Wants To Go To Fairyland?

Who wants to go to FAIRY LAND with me?
This is a place only the invisible can see.

Fairyland is a country of golden dreams
Where children reign as Kings and Queens.
Within each heart – we remain
Prince, Princess, girl and boy.
Purity of innocence and joy.
Never substituted by a toy.

This is a place where Wizards and Dragons live forever
With ancient power and splendid treasure.
Heroes win by virtue of trial and endeavor
Brave and bold or… being clever.
To encounter nightmare monsters of our fears
Our regrets and lonely tears
Chances and circumstances unforeseen
Yet strangers—we have never been.

Adventure calls and we shall ride
Our shaggy ponies side by side
Wade the rivers deep and wide
Through oak forests where the elven hide
Mushrooms our passengers and our mystic guides.
Strange cacti, vines, and spore,
Make the spirit eagle soar.

The guardian if he comes at all,
So fey, thin and tall
Known by legend and by song
As the Pied Piper at the gates of dawn.

His songs are ancient secrets of enchanted lands
Shining silver waters and golden sand
Mermaid mirrors and seashell fans

Magic spells and wishing wells
Stories that the fables tell,
Strands of deeper meanings made
Nature spoken and displayed.

Majestic whales the wisdom of the ocean hold
Narwhals, unicorns never bought or sold.
Elephants, incarnated kings of old
Myths can say what must be told.

What is false and what is truth?
Time reveals and documents the proof.
Not all fantasy is fantasy
Not all rhymes are poetry.

If Fairyland does not exist
It is still my favorite place to visit.

Wildflowers In The Alley

Little children with sticky hands, dusty naked feet under rags
Big brown eyes, fat baby cheeks, hair tousled
Smiling, jostling, laughing…begging
Outside the restaurants waiting for left-overs
Scraps from the plates of tourists…
Shooed away by the waiters with anxious faces.
Shy smiles and giggles—a tourist sneaks a treat to them.
Perhaps this tiny girl—will be sold
When she learns not to cry anymore.
Older boys will die from sniffing glue.
Not even eleven years old—they die in dumpsters.
Wildflowers unnoticed,
Ragged petals in an alley, unwanted
Plucked from the garden of poverty,
A mother's desperate need
A state or religion that allows no advice or help to women…
The abandoned children shooed away from the full plates
Of the affluent, the tourists, the hard faced men.
"Pro-lifer" condemns poor women for her crime of pregnancy.

O Lord, Won't You Buy
Me an Ol' Chevy Truck

(A Country-Western Song)

O Lordy, won't cha buy me an ol' Chevy truck
At home I hate to be stuck.
I can't go to the mall or the store,
I can't stand to watch the kids anymore.
They play the same reruns on the TV
There are so many places I'd rather be.

O Lordy, if you buy me an ol' Chevy truck
I don't care which model
I don't care which year
I'll make the payments, Lord
If you buy the beer!

If I had an ol' Chevy truck
I'd drive real careful
I'd drive real slow
And watch for pedestrians
Where ever I go.
I'll even play gospel music on the ol' radio!

O Lord, Won't Cha Get Me A Boyfriend!

O Lord, won't cha get me a boyfriend
With class and with style
Someone with his own teeth, Lord
That shine when he smile…
Someone who has a job, Lord
Doing something worthwhile.
Somebody who don't leave
His clothes in a pile!

My ol' boyfriend borrows my money
He'll never repay
Eats all my groceries
His friends don't go away.

My ol' boyfriend eats his soup with a fork
Sucks on his moustache
Don't go to work
Sleeps with is boots on
Snores like a hog.
I think I'll go to the pound, Lord
And get me a dog.

At the Museum of Natural History—they say
There's a missing link,
No, he hain't missin'
Not even close to extinct
He's merely passed out
Underneath my kitchen sink.
I'll even donate the stuff that he drink!

To My Friend In Prison

Herod awaits thy birth with fear and scorn...
To murder thee as soon as thou art born.
Thy life blown hence by ill fortune's breath
As war would hasten youthful injury or death...

What merit in this life we lead?
As we blame—as we are blamed
Lied to, deceived by wrongs
Dreadful roots, to this life belongs.

Our flaws, mistakes, or faults
Called to justify for present ill
Injustice and indifference in gestalt
Thy rules and laws that they fulfill...

Victims, martyrs are chosen so
People sacrifice a future to status-quo
Christ, crucified, the world's loss
Branded with the shame
Of a criminal upon the cross...

Do not drown thy heart in bitterness
Against thy fellow men
Nor be by their sins distressed
Steady thyself to become like Christ on Earth
(Illumined by the glory of Heaven's worth.)

Of freedom thou art by laws bereft
In life—there is no freedom left
By constant prayer and a saintly life
Bring thee safety from this worldly strife.

Humble-hearted with thy sorrow
Raise thy mind to a greater morrow
A life lived gently with deep thought
Forgives thy youthful deeds by folly wrought.

Contemplation and peace after trial
Contentment without anger or denial
Freedom lives inside the soul as well as out
When freedom is from hunger, worry, doubt.

Consider now the human condition
Each life is tested by fateful decision
Some for better, some for worse, in a situation.
Comfort thy soul by comforting others
(Truly all mortals here—are our brothers.

Eve And Adam

Adam (A-damn spelled backwards is Mad-a)
Tattled upon Eve, Adam projected the blame
Scandal and shame!
We know she was innocent
We know she was framed...
(Because backwards or forwards her name is spelled the same.)

She had nothing to gain
She trusted Adam
(Or the snake under his fig leaf)
Like most women
(She believed in true love and romance)
She had no defender (no lawyer)
So she fell in the trap
She took the whole rap
For all Adam's crap.

Besides, there were no witnesses
We know the snake—he always lies...
So condemned forever
No trial, no jury to recall
Thus women were blamed
For mankind's fall.
Poor Eve—un-thanked
Mother of us all.

Thus Priest, Church, King, Patriarchal Power was gained
The Garden of Eden exploited and tamed.
Trade Paradise for traffic, freeways, ghettoes, prisons, and fear
Christmas commercials, TV and beer.

The wonder and beauty—the natural and nude
Jokes about women often mean or crude.
A Saint's temptation to resist women—to refuse a kiss.
All appreciation of women ignored or dismissed.

The Priest, the Prude, the Pope, and the Square
What do those guys really care?
Jealous of the love they do not share…
They go home alone to their cold beds
And rule the world with violence instead.
Each prayer ends with "AHHH-MEN"
Sounds like a lament for the original sin.

Thus day after day, they war against women
They war against nature…
In their power—the world doth burn
Until someday the Gates of Eden return…
We will return to love's innocence
With experience gained.

Adam will be Tarzan
And Eve will be Jane.
With a warm and cheerful light

Requiem

A blazing hoop of white, Sun rules a barren land
While moon rides the shadows of the night
Gating over the desert rocks and sand.
Stars on quiet Wings, a million fairy lights
Constellations glittering and move
Across wide spaces of the night.
Mesquite trees are twisted low, silhouetted against the sky.
Devil winds fiercely blow the grasses, burnt and dry.
Wild horses run on open plains
Raising dusty clouds
They are wild as storm and rain
Hooves beat the earth like drums
Space and light are all they claim
All their hearts as one.
Their heritage is freedom.

A stallion shakes out his tangled mane
His tail sweeps the ground.
A warrior's heart beats within his muscled frame
As he leads his mustang herd around
Through many hardships long sustained.
Huddled among companions -
The mustangs at night hold
The stallion watching over them
Their bodies warm against the cold.

This warrior's heart is troubled
He dances like a winter flame
His nostrils quiver. He shivers with a sudden.

Dark wings are drawn to him. They circle closer still.
A blaze of headlights and sounds of motors break the silence.
Dust makes a rolling cloud.
Men close in to the left — they steal to the right.
A helicopter swirls in from the sky aloud.
First fire bursts into the startled horses' eyes
It panics the herd. The stallion's scream splits the skies asunder.
Astonished by the blades of tempest wind
Noises to them that sounds like thunder.
Whence come the enemy - the lethal stranger
Man, the mortal danger.
Men raise their weapons
The stallion's ears lie flat upon his head.
His hooves strike out like hammers on the jeeps.
He soars over the barricade of man's defenses
He is no prisoner of fences
"SHOOT' SHOOT HIM" Men shout
The stallion whirls about.
Two men climb the sides of their truck in fear.
As the stallion steals his closest companions!

The stallion to his harem calls
A high-powered rifle shot
The smoking gun
The stallion rears and falls
He screams out in pain and warning
The herd panics in confusion.
The horses attempt to stampede.

The Stallion falls screaming to the ground.
Men beat and bludgeon horses
With iron clubs and gun
Wounded horses are driven down
Upon their bloody knees
A vulture's feast
Blind eye staring at the sun.

What victory is won by violence?
What death worthy or the price?
In the dust there is a symbol dying
Who gains by this bloody sacrifice?

Man may claim dominion
Over earth and sea
He puts his world in a prison
By random acts of cruelty.
They may speak or freedom
When freedom — it is dying…
But when they speak of freedom
They surely must be lying.
Wild horses are the living freedom
Where man can never go
Contained by four square walls
A freedom man shall never know
But wild mustangs run no more
The wind reclaims it's own
Buffalo and bear are gone
There is blood upon the Stone.
In the distance of the mountains
Lightning flashes bright
Cloulds are piled silver

Cloulds feel agreed with light
Listen to their hose like heartbeats
Children of the wind are galloping
Like thunder through the night

Praise For A Despised And Feared Insect

She dances in air
Upon fractal filaments
Finer than a hair —
Invisible zip-line
To anywhere.
She pivots on mathematics
Engineering and design.
She diagrams the ethers
Precision in each line
Her art is ingenious
Mysterious and sublime.
She scribbles seraphic texts
In a calligraphy of daring arabesques.
A weaver and a hunter
Self-employed
Trapeze artist, spiral dancer
Weft and orb.
By her labors self-absorbed.
Ultimate as stalker, universally feared
Said to eat her lovers
Notoriously weird.

Her gestures ritualistic
Primordial in her skill
Purposefully one - minded
Cold - hearted in her kill.

Her attachments are made from universal glue
She connects the edges of the existing with the new
She creates an optical geometry
Diamond bracelets of early morning dew.
She wove the first basket
She invented the dream-catcher too.

She wraps her victims like Egyptian mummies
When they are dead
She sleeps in a hammock -
She eats her breakfast in bed.
Native legend says: Spider wove a cosmic net
To protect the Earth from the comets as they fell.
She organized their orbits, sent the bad one's home
In darkness now - those pesky comets dwell.
She is exiled to a small corner of your house
A solitary insect
All she asks is to be left alone.

Once - she was beautiful
Now she is shy
Perhaps embarrassed
To look so hideous to the human eye.
Cursed by Athena, a Greek Goddess
In a fit of jealousy…
Once there was a great contest
To prove which weaver was the best.
Held by Greek Goddess Athene, a weaver's patroness
They stole Arachne's loom and her thread
Arachne - ever resourceful
Used eight fingers for her loom
She spun her own hair — to create the finest web

A web so fine -it was invisible to see
This provoked ATHENA'S jealousy
Before the Weaver's Contest
Arachne was a beautiful Princess
When Arachne won
Athena cursed her to become hideous
To be feared and despised by everyone.
Punished for her resourcefulness —
Because she was the best.

Princess Arachne lived long ago in a palace
On an island called Crete.
She saved a Greek hero (Athena's pet human)
When he was lost in a dark labyrinth
She gave the man a string to guide him out.
Arachne protected him from a monster called a Minotaur
(Minotaur had the enormous head of a bull.)
Arachne fell in love With the Greek hero -
She begged to go with him upon his ship.
But the man she loved (whom she had saved)
Was already married, so he left her on a desert island
Far away from home
She was pregnant and alone.
He abandoned her to starve and die
The only way she could stay alive
Was to eat his child — to survive.
For this reason - she is hostile to men…
Sometimes poisonous to them
Spider is Arachne, Spider Woman,
It is the reason why…
Forever cursed, she is strange and shy…

Once when Spirit ruled the World — Beauty Was!

NOT the possession of any man or tribe...
Foreign Men began to steal what was not his
His fences contain fields
Fields become ranch or farm or mine
The world broken into pieces
Eternity divided into time.
Miners came with dynamite
Farmers with claws of iron, knives of steel
Ranchers with their rifles
Selfish each of their own exclusive right
To fashion the vastness to their like
For gold and silver and other things
They stake their worldly claims
Men died for greed and gain
And they call it "Civilization".

Like a battle of a war...
They said West was Won
Railroaders killed the Buffalo and Mustangs
Fences imprison all the fertile land
European cows and cattle - drudges for our meat
A symbol of tame servitude
Symbolic of man's exploitation and defeat.
On this Continent of Freedom
From sea to shining sea
We never see an antelope...

No wolves in the great forests howl...
Poisons kill the birds, butterflies, and bee...

Royalty Of Trees

Early evening gloaming
Wolf moon rises over the horizon — full and bright.
Ice glistens like reflections in glass windows
Etched by cold refraction's of the white.
Lakes are ballrooms crystallized in silver
Where veiled brides dance in prismed light.
Trees quiver with every gusty blow.
Oaks are wearing hoary garments
Heads crowned by mistletoe.
Their palace is hidden in the forest
A grove festooned with snow...
Lofty cedars wave their tassled sleeves
They curtsy to the tall knights of noble pine,
Their white hoop skirts brush a sequined floor.
Boughs are laced with frost and embroidered fine
Delicate brocades of branches rustle
Wave with grand and graceful gestures
Like royal kings and queens of yore.
Trees spire like church steeples,
High processions are lit by diamond shine
The glitter of icey stars and moon light
In a Cathedral of the Divine.

Conversation With W.B. Yeats

As I read those Druid haunted phrases
Ringing with the echoes of an ancient temple bell
Words levitate in the exquisite way of hummingbirds
Elevate the mind until words swell with primal images
And leap across the page to the of our rhymes
Sure and swift as stag or doe
Taut as the string of a hunter's bow
Verse is terse.
Nothing trips the tongue so well
As the speeches we rehearse
Until words could not be better said.
We converse one poet to another
Although I'm alive and you are dead…
Upon the kisses of our Muse
Both of us have fed
Your works immortal
As long as great poets are revered and read.
While I am beginning to be heard.
You left the garden untended here for me
To clear the paths for this new century.

We lost our ears to hear the Earth
A trillion eyes are blind
All the places we departed from
All the ones we left behind…
Where are the places we began?
Our lost mysteries divine...
What it is or what it means
Do we understand or can we define?
We are secrets of Eternity
We are plenitudes unsung..
A person is a moment's dream
Nature is never done...
The souls of mankind
Are hardly lost or won,,.
When we do not know the reality
Of this heart and mind.

Krishna and Shiva dance

That's a good idea.
Flowers and fruit on the alters.
Krishna is beautiful.
Shiva has panache.

At least when Krishna lived
His people didn't crucify him.
Go ahead and call them "heathen" or "idol worshipper".

At least they aren't "idle worshippers"
Sitting in pews hardly awake
And going out the next day
To work killing something.

I think Jesus Krishna
With a different story.
A different culture.
God can come down more than once.
Are the Jews the only ones?

But let's learn to love
Each other and love God
In every different way.

The Omen

On the road to Damascus
Paul was struck blind
By a Fiery Light
The Angel of the Lord spoke
And Paul was a changed
And chastened man…

Today a fiery explosion
Lit the night sky like a sudden day
Damascus Arkansas
A Titan 2 Missile Silo exploded
There was a nuclear warhead
The Pentagon says was fortunately not damaged
Altho' twenty—two men were injured
And a thousand people were evacuated
From Damascus and Gravesville…

The warning is clear
The Angel of the Lord has spoken here
When Lord speaks
Some hear thunder
Some see the Light.

Fable Of A Candle

Here is my little candle
To show the way I came
I take care to guard it
from ignorance, fear, and shame.
I paid a high price for it
In experience and pain
Because each time it blew out
I was lost again.

Now I watch it carefully
Flickering through the wind and rain
I defend it – the best I can...
From the monsters in my brain.
There is no-where I can run
To hide would be in vain...
If I can face my fear
Monsters I might tame..

Along the path if we should meet
On mountainside or street.
Although Our paths may differ
Our faces may look different
Each called a different name
But the light that shines within us
The light is just the same.

Each candle is our guide
Perhaps all we ever call our own.
Yet one candle seems so dim alone
Perhaps by the light of two or more
We can find our way back home.

Someday, when this journey is Over
Perhaps we'll meet again
Where all the candles circle
To make a golden chain.
Flames dance in many colors.

Rays are bright and clear
They make of Heaven
A glowing chandelier.....
Which could blind us with its glory
If we came. too near.

So again to darkness
We nestle down to rest
No fear is in the darkness now
The darkness now we bless
The darkness is our pillow
Our Mother's loving breast.

The candle is just a metaphor
With weak and timid glow.
As we stumble along the road
This world we can never know.
Let our laughter share our sorrow
Where-ever we may go.
May our knowledge become wisdom

Great with understanding may it grow…

Dear Friend and Fellow Pilgrim
Take this candle shining bright
May it help you on the path
With a warm and cheerful light.

The quest that lies before you
Is the quest for your own soul.
Its purpose will reveal itself
Its purpose will unfold.

We must have courage and be brave
We must be true of heart and bold.
Or when we weary of the battle
Will we surrender to the cold?

The fear of darkness
Of all the things invisible to our sight.
May be full of miracles
Not just the Monsters that we fight.

Until you return
Let your candle burn….
Give your darkness to the light
And send your soul like a flaming arrow
Into the dark beauty of the night.
This poem is dedicated to all spiritual seekers

In gratitude to **HERMES CATON**, *Theosophist,*
Beacon Lodge, San Diego, CA.

The Banana Eating Republic

Why do they say apes are Our ancestors?
Cousin to the chimp
Aunt Ouragutang
Brother-in-law of the lemur
Step-son of a spider monkey?

Those large eyed and long tailed
wrinkled brow
anxiously picking nits from fur
tenderly holding a fuzzy
so innocent and mischievous
we must fall in love with them.

Why do men prefer to be to the simian?
Is it an excuse
For being stupid, violent or sexual?
How did we lose that wonderful prehensile tail
- the pride of the banana eating republic
With wrinkled fingers
and eternal wisdom
Of monkey magic in their eyes.

Are you good enough to be one of THEM?
Don't you envy their freedom?
Aren't you just jealous of the ability
To swing from a tree branch
With a curled tail?

Easter Poem For Animals

The one called our Savior, He who was crucified
For his body and blood – as sacrifice for us he died
Everyday animals are sacrificed – slaughtered
Here we go again — man's arrogance and profit glorified
Consumers of death — we have innocence despised
By Science and Religion — animal sentience denied.

Bless God's children — God's creation everywhere
Bless the people who respect, who care
Bless them who rescue, heal, and they, who defend
All God's innocent children — who are truly our friends
May the divine mercy of Christ be granted to them.

Who knows the flight of an eagle?
Who hears the thoughts of a tree?
Who seeks to set all wild things free?
Who hears the wolves howling far away - out of sight,
Far from strip malls, highways, and city's bright lights?
Where the Milky Way and Constellations glow in the night.
These are the values of a Spirit at peace.
For the troubles we face - may our souls be released.

Bless God's children — the creatures everywhere
Bless them who help and who care
For the world and for this blue planet we share
Bless the people who shelter. feed, and defend
All God's Children — who give their lives for us
May the divine mercy Of Christ be granted to them.

The Calico Cat

I am a calico cat with big green eyes,
Sophisticated, elegant, and supernaturally wise.
I have long tale (some truth and some lies)
But am silent with secrets, I don't compromise.
I leap for a shelf and if it topples and falls,
I pretend no surprise,
As a matter of fact - I meant to do that.
I'm agile — I survive… besides- I have 8 more lives.

They worshipped me in Egypt, there - I was a deity.
Remember me in Old Siam? There -I am still royalty.
I expect respect from my human servants.
You open a can of cat-food for me.
When my eyes are dosed — my nose can see.
Is that a tuna sandwich —you'll share with me?
At the twitch of my tail all vermin turn pale.
If my ears are asleep — my whiskers can hear.
All the rats tremble with fear.
I'll bring you my toy—a big juicy mouse
You may as well know now - how I rule this house.

Cameron Ranch In Campo

An acorn worked twiggy fingers
through fissured boulders
by prodigious efforts towards sun.
Oak brawny shoulders
Pushed through the granite slab.

In the decades that followed
cradled by the mother stone,
warmed by sun in rocky veins
It hears the disputes of mountains
with all their windy claims.

Far in the background are the soldiers,
Low of cattle and the trains.
Wildfires scorched the edges
of its harsh domain.

Conflicting desert winds
hold battles on the airy field.
Harsh and cold or dry and thin
An ancient war that none ever win.
Sometimes they break the brittle elbows
of these plain outspoken limbs.

The oak lifts its rough and homely face
to quiet fields and watching cliffs
from its hard won place
Outstretched shaggy arms

welcome canopy of noonday rest
for cows and crows
and other guests…

Eloquent in wordless ways
This oak says to me:
"By persistence faith is won
Despair and hardship overcome."
For twenty years I've passed this tree
That grows from bedrock
It gives me hope, that I find
this faith and strength also in me.

In My Garden

Low growing fuzzy chamomile
soft silver mullein leaves
clovers bound
Like wooly balls
Up the rocks
And down…

Dancing in the breeze
In light harmony
Gracefully at ease
Nodding to one another
As if they all agree.

The tall and short
dark with bright
Singing cheerful morning songs
Lilting towards afternoon
Drowsy with the humming of the bees.

Evening comes in tie-dyed clouds
Serves informal teas
Flowers close their petals up
To her soft melodies.

Night is a formal affair
Dark satin coats and velvet gown
Diamonds in her crown.

The main attraction is the moon
Each night he wears a different costume
He takes another shape
Every night he lights up the stage
And plays a different tune.

Dreamtime In The Mountain Empire

They say there a cavern under the cracked dam at the lake
before the City drained Lake Morena into Otay Lakes
and left us with barely 10% of the water
that we need to keep the Oaks alive
ruining the fishing and tourism
water to put out frequent border fires between us and Mexico.
Be that as it may — nothing we could do legally.

In Hauzer Canyon - The Mountain Lion is King.
The King is invisible — no one ever sees him/
He is faster than a speeding bullet and so secret is his lair.
Let me begin
About this big cavern
where the Mountain Spirits lives...
Some guy tells me in a hushed whispers
"The stones are crystals as big as trucks
cool and clear as ice
hanging from the ceiling like chandeliers…"
"Black water sky — with tiny stars twinkling
Like Mica in obsidian."

He said There are blind fish…
Fish as white as paper swimming in the underground pools,,."
I asked "How do you know they are blind?"
He said the fish have no eyes.
He told me that if a ray of moonlight

pierces the darkness like a spear...
That ray of moonlight never returns to the moon
but is lost forever.!
"If blind white fish and mountain lions live inside the cavern
below the dam in Hauzer Canyon
how about bats, bugs, owls and snakes?" I asked
"Spirits in their temporary physical animal forms"... he replied
"The Spirits banished from and by your culture...
Exiled from your Churches
Forgotten in the graveyards of our ancestors."

I was in the cavern, in a dream, a long time ago
A Spirit beckoned me to an open stone door.
Beyond the stone door was a beautiful valley...
sunlit and marvelously green
Sometimes I get so homesick that I cry

Mustangs

Swirling blades and wheels in the sky
Stampede the wild horses, terrified
Stallions rise on their hooves
TO defend the herd
Mares break and run
Colts trampled in the panic.

They are herded into metal pens
Separated by rank, age, and gender
Men poke their captives with sharp sticks
or electric prods..
To rouse the drooping heads
and skinny flanks.
Leaving them to rot
In industrial metal tanks.

Prisoners of BLM
At the bequest or the demand
Of the wealthy Association of Cattlemen
Expenses paid by your taxation.
BLM auctions off the horses
To foreign men for slaughter.
Each death for a bit of forage
And for polluted water.

Convicted of the crime of freedom
The crime of not being tame.
The anguish of innocence.
TO languish in a crowded dirty pen.

Where many rule —
None take the blame.
Freedom crucified
By treachery, secrets, lies.
Some say freedom in America
Is only the freedom that you buy.

Horses Sold For Slaughter

Foreign men with cold quicksilver eyes
Willing to buy cheap souls for slaughter…
Those chosen will not be tamed – nor given reins
Charged by Cattlemen for foraging and water.
Helicopters round up herds for them
Stampede the panicked mustangs
Into dead-end traps of the BLM
Acting as agents of the Cattlemen.

Wild horses languish in the yard
Under petty malice of the hired men
Men pry and poke them with sham sticks
Each horse locked into metal pens
Drooping heads and skinny flanks
Each Soul of Freedom thereby fell
Into the dominion of man's power.
Tedium serves his master well
Suffering - slowly passing hours.
Inmates of a living Hell
By heat, cold, filthy water, moldy hay
Free Spririt dies – a captive.

Blood and meat are nothing more
When there is no freedom left to live.
Death - the only choice
Hypocrisy is sly — to cover a corruption
Wheeling, dealing legalized stealing
Where many rule – none accept the blame

Climate controlled in quiet luxury of sterile offices
Memos are written with cold unconcerned conceit
Invisible - the suffering of wild horses
Prisoners of words and "good intentions"
Prisoners of docile deceit…!

Ugliness has many servants
To destroy the wild, brave, and free
Motivated by a secret envy or jealousy
—From man's heart that has no vision
Hearts so blind they cannot see,
The rightful heirs of beauty and raw power
The courage of untamed Spirit
-All that drab bureaucrats can never be

The wild horse is a guest of a great land
Noble lord of the lone prairies.
National treasure made by God's own hand.
And the cattle are more like disease.

For The Price Of A Unicorn

Suffering horses — slow passing days.
Inmates of misery – innocents in Hell
By heat, cold, filthy water, moldy hay
Captive Spirits — prisoners — defenseless
Tedium this master well
And death is lengthened by delay.

They Who dispose of another's freedom
All freedoms - mock and revile
Forest Service kill roaming buffalo and wolves
Taking orders from the Ranchers,
As bribes mock Democracy
All freedom - corruption defiles,
Where many rule — none takes the blame...
Officials take orders from whom it pays to please

Ugly kills the Beautiful
Tame would kill the Free
Prisons made for crimes of Men
Not meant for innocents as these.
While cattle in the wilderness
Are more like a filthy disease.
Cattle trample and tear the earth —
Until nothing is left, but stink
Cows pollute the water
That other creatures need to drink.

Courthouse Blues

They say there is no more slavery
They say all men are free.
Pardon me dear Citizen
If I should disagree.

Vindictive and Convictive is the Court of Law
Where Judges rule from Golden Thrones
Upon the mice in beds of straw…
Upon the head of Able
They brand the mark of Cain
To disable the Able
With a fable
For the sake of their own gain.
They use the word "justice"
To make a guilt machine.
Lawyers and Attorneys
Ask: How do plead, son?
How much innocence can you afford, today?
Can you pay my fee?
This is the price for each man's liberty
Mass incarceration for peons and for peasants
Then oppress the rest with warrants for their arrest
While the jury screams freedom for "Barabas."

Domination and Dominion
Replaces truth with an opinion.
Uses a secret jargon and threats into the bargain
Your hard-earned cash - they steal your stash.
While the real criminals get away.

Easter Poem For Animals

The one called our Savior, He who was crucified
For his body and blood — as sacrifice for us he died
Everyday animals are sacrificed - slaughtered
Here we go again — man's arrogance and profit glorified
Consumers of death — we have innocence despised
By Science and Religion — animal sentience denied.

Bless God's children — God's creation everywhere
Bless the people who respect, who care
Bless them who rescue, heal, and they who defend
All God's innocent children — who are truly our friends
May the divine mercy of Christ be granted to them.

Who knows the flight of an eagle?
Who hears the thoughts of a tree?
Who seeks to set all wild things free?
Who hears the wolves howling far away - out of sight?
Far from strip malls, highways, and city's bright lights.
Where the Milky Way and Constellations glow in the night.
These are the values of a Spirit at peace.
For the troubles we face - may our souls be released.

Bless God's children — the creatures everywhere
Bless them who help and who care
For the world and for this blue planet we share
Bless the people who shelter. feed, and defend
All God's Children — who give their lives for us
May the divine mercy of Christ be granted to them.